diary girl notes

Share great news, your latest
mood, or just make plans
for the weekend.
Tear out a note & fold on the
dotted line. Seal it with a
cool sticker & pass it
to a groovy
girlfriend.

diary girl™ notes

Written and illustrated by
Mickey Gill and Cheryl Biddix

FINE print
PUBLISHING

Fine Print Publishing Company
P.O. Box 916401
Longwood, Florida 32971-6401

ISBN 1-892951-31-2

Write us.
We would love
to hear from
you.

STOP BY
OUR WEBSITE

www.diarygirl.com

Find cool books to
share between friends
and diaries to keep your
secrets safe.

diary
girl

Nov 8/05

Today, I'm feeling ✓ Sweet ❀ Sour

Saturday, let's ✓ go to the mall ❀ hang out @ my house ✓ only eat ice cream

❀ Memorize contents ❀ Make note disappear ❀ Share with _____.

Folding without thumbs is too hard!

diary girl

diarygirl.com

diary
girl

If 2day were a color, it would _____.

This note is sort of a secret · Open 2 the public

Need 2 no info · Tell me what U think · Here's the sitch

diary
girl

diarygirl.com

diary girl

⭐ I've been dying to tell U! ⭐ Sneak peek ⭐ This is hot!

⭐ Thought U should no ⭐ Keep this 2 yourself ⭐ Not so private

You're ● such a princess ● a wild child ● groovy

diary
girl

Got any homework I can eat?

 wish _____.

Chew on this   Inside scoop   U won't  lieve it!

Feed this to your 🐾 after reading   Send me a note

I command U 2 fold this 4 me!

diary girl

diarygirl.com

You don't expect a princess 2 fold, do you?

diary
girl
diarygirl.com

diary girl

👁 think _____ is cute!

🗑 this after reading   For your 👁👁 only

Write back asap   e-mail me L8er   Pass on 2 _____

diarygirl.com

diary
girl

You can never be too glamorous.

👁 **Need** 🐾 a new dress 🐾 a fairy godmother 🐾 glass slippers

🐾 Get your 🐾 🐾 on this! 🐾 Tell me what U think

🐾 Pugs & kisses 🐾 Best friends furever

diary girl

Greetings from ⬡ 🗼 ⬡ Mars ⬡ _____ class

This is ⬡ Super exclusive ⬡ Top secret ⬡ The worst!

U R so ⬡ Outtasite ⬡ Crazy (in a cool way) ⬡ Amazing

diary
girl
diarygirl.com

diary girl

_____ is so yummy!

U won't 🐝 lieve what I know!   Private or   public knowledge

Leave a note in my locker   Call my 📱 L8er

diary girl

♔ If I were queen, I would _____

♥ Didja no?   ♥ Here's the lowdown   ♥ Crazy good!   ♥ This is hot!

♥ Talk 2 U tomorrow   ♥ Meet me @_____between classes

diary
girl

diarygirl.com

diary
girl

Today, I'm feeling  Sweet Sour

Saturday, let's go to the mall hang out @ my house only eat ice cream

Memorize contents Make note disappear Share with _____.

diary
girl

If 2day were a color, it would _____.

This note is sort of a secret   Open 2 the public

Need 2 no info   Tell me what U think   Here's the sitch

diary
girl

diarygirl.com

diary girl

⭐ I've been dying to tell U!   ⭐ Sneak peek   ⭐ This is hot!

⭐ Thought U should no   ⭐ Keep this 2 yourself   ⭐ Not so private

You're ⬤ such a princess   ⬤ a wild child   ⬤ groovy

diary
girl

Got any homework I can eat?

👁 wish _____

⭐ Chew on this   ⭐ Inside scoop   ⭐ U won't 🐝 lieve it!

⭐ Feed this to your after reading   ⭐ Send me a note

I command
U 2 fold
this 4 me!

diary
girl

diarygirl.com

diary
girl

Call my land line   IM me tonight

Reply to sender   Just between U & me   Not a secret

Daydreaming about   shopping   a crush   having a party

diary girl

👁 think _____ is cute!

🗑 this after reading 🌸 For your 👀 only

🌸 Write back asap 🌸 e-mail me L8er 🌸 Pass on 2 _____

diary girl

You can never be too glamorous.

👁 **Need** a new dress   a fairy godmother   glass slippers

Get your 🐾 🐾 on this!   Tell me what U think

Pugs & kisses   Best friends furever

diary
girl
diarygirl.com

diary
girl

Greetings from ( ) 🗼 ( ) Mars ( ) _____ class

This is 🌸 Super exclusive 🌸 Top secret 🌸 The worst!

U R so 🌸 Outtasite 🌸 Crazy (in a cool way) 🌸 Amazing

diary girl

_____ is so yummy!

U won't bee lieve what I know!   Private or 🌸 public knowledge

Leave a note in my locker   Call my 📱 L8er

diarygirl.com

diary girl

♕ If I were queen, I would _____

♥ Didja no?   ♥ Here's the lowdown   ♥ Crazy good!   ♥ This is hot!

♥ Talk 2 U tomorrow   ♥ Meet me @_____between classes

diary
girl
diarygirl.com

diary girl

Today, I'm feeling ✿ Sweet ✿ Sour

Saturday, let's ✿ go to the mall ✿ hang out @ my house ✿ only eat ice cream

✿ Memorize contents ✿ Make note disappear ✿ Share with _____.

folding without thumbs is too hard!

diary
girl

diarygirl.com

diary
girl

If 2day were a color, it would _____ .

This note is sort of a secret

Open 2 the public

Need 2 no info

Tell me what U think

Here's the sitch

diary
girl

★ I've been dying to tell U! ★ Sneak peek ★ This is hot!

★ Thought U should no ★ Keep this 2 yourself ★ Not so private

You're ● such a princess ● a wild child ● groovy

diary
girl

Got any homework I can eat?

★ 👁 wish _____.

★ Chew on this ★ Inside scoop ★ U won't 🐝lieve it!

★ Feed this to your 🐕 after reading ★ Send me a note

diarygirl.com

diary
girl

👁 think _____ is cute!

🗑 this after reading   For your 👀👀 only

Write back asap   e-mail me L8er   Pass on 2 _____

Fold this 4 me and I'll let you wear my tiara!

diary
girl

diarygirl.com

diary girl

You can never be too glamorous.

Need a new dress a fairy godmother glass slippers

Get your 🐾 👀 on this! Tell me what U think

Pugs & kisses Best friends furever

diary girl

Greetings from ◯ Paris ◯ Mars ◯ _____ class

This is ◯ Super exclusive ◯ Top secret ◯ The worst!

U R so ◯ Outtasite ◯ Crazy (in a cool way) ◯ Amazing

diary
girl

diarygirl.com

diary girl

_____ is so yummy!

U won't bee lieve what I know!   Private or   public knowledge

Leave a note in my locker   Call my   L8er

diary girl

If I were queen, I would _____

♥ Didja no?   ♥ Here's the lowdown   ♥ Crazy good!   ♥ This is hot!

♥ Talk 2 U tomorrow   ♥ Meet me @_____between classes

diary girl

Today, I'm feeling ✿ Sweet ✿ Sour

Saturday, let's ✿ go to the mall ✿ hang out @ my house ✿ only eat ice cream

✿ Memorize contents ✿ Make note disappear ✿ Share with _____.

Folding
without
thumbs is
too hard!

diary
girl
diarygirl.com

diary
girl

If 2day were a color, it would _____.

This note is sort of a secret   Open 2 the public

Need 2 no info   Tell me what U think   Here's the sitch

Can U fold this 4 me? My nails R still wet.

diary
girl
diarygirl.com

diary girl

⭐ I've been dying to tell U! ⭐ Sneak peek ⭐ This is hot!

⭐ Thought U should no ⭐ Keep this 2 yourself ⭐ Not so private

You're ● such a princess ● a wild child ● groovy

Have U seen my glass slipper?

diary
girl
diarygirl.com

diary
girl

Got any homework I can eat?

★ 👁 wish _____.

Chew on this ★ Inside scoop ★ U won't 🐝 lieve it!

Feed this to your 🐶 after reading ★ Send me a note

diarygirl.com

diary
girl

○ Call my land line ○ IM me tonight
○ Reply to sender ○ Just between U & me ○ Not a secret
Daydreaming about ○ shopping ○ a crush ○ having a party

diary girl

diarygirl.com

diary girl

✿ 👁 think _____ is cute!

✿ 🗑 this after reading   ✿ For your 👀 👀 only

✿ Write back asap   ✿ e-mail me L8er   ✿ Pass on 2 _____

Fold this 4 me and I'll let you wear my tiara!

diarygirl.com

diary girl

You can never be too glamorous.

👁 **Need** a new dress a fairy godmother glass slippers

Get your 🐾 🐾 on this! Tell me what U think

Pugs & kisses Best friends furever

Can U fold this 4 me? My nails R still wet.

diary girl

diarygirl.com

diary girl

Greetings from ◯ 🗼 ◯ Mars ◯ _____ class

This is ◯ Super exclusive ◯ Top secret ◯ The worst!

U R so ◯ Outtasite ◯ Crazy (in a cool way) ◯ Amazing

diary
girl

_____ is so yummy!

U won't lieve what I know!   Private or 🌸 public knowledge

🌸 Leave a note in my locker   Call my 📱 L8er

diary girl

👑
If I were queen, I would _____

💛 Didja no?   💛 Here's the lowdown   💛 Crazy good!   💛 This is hot!

💛 Talk 2 U tomorrow   💛 Meet me @_____between classes

diary girl

Today, I'm feeling 🌸 Sweet 🌸 Sour

Saturday, let's 🌸 go to the mall 🌸 hang out @ my house 🌸 only eat ice cream

🌸 Memorize contents 🌸 Make note disappear 🌸 Share with _____.

Folding without thumbs is too hard!

diary girl

diarygirl.com

diary girl

If 2day were a color, it would _____.

This note is sort of a secret

Open 2 the public

Need 2 no info

Tell me what U think

Here's the sitch

diary
girl

diarygirl.com

diary
girl

★ I've been dying to tell U! ★ Sneak peek ★ This is hot!

★ Thought U should no ★ Keep this 2 yourself ★ Not so private

You're ● such a princess ● a wild child ● groovy

diarygirl.com

diary girl

Got any homework I can eat?

 wish _____.

Chew on this   Inside scoop   U won't lieve it!

Feed this to your 🐶 after reading   Send me a note

I command
U 2 fold
this 4 me!

diary
girl

diarygirl.com

diary
girl

Call my land line ● IM me tonight ●

Reply to sender ● Just between U & me ● Not a secret ●

Daydreaming about ● shopping ● a crush ● having a party

diarygirl.com

diary
girl

✿ 👁 think _____ is cute!

✿ 🗑 this after reading ✿ For your 👁 👁 only

✿ Write back asap ✿ e-mail me L8er ✿ Pass on 2 _____